101 CRUCIAL LESSONS
THEY DON'T TEACH YOU IN
BUSINESS SCHOOL

---

by Chris Haroun

Also written by Chris Haroun:

"The Ultimate Practical Business Manual
Everything You Need to Know About Business
(from Launching a Company to Taking it Public)"

101 Crucial Lessons They Don't Teach you in Business School

Copyright © 2015 by Chris Haroun

Second Printed Edition

(Published by www.BusinessCareerCoaching.com)

Dedication

To my Mom and Dad who gave me the faith and confidence to know in my heart that you can accomplish anything in life.

Purpose of this Book / About the Author

Chris Haroun has had the opportunity in his career to meet with the top CEOs, entrepreneurs and investors in the world, including Warren Buffett, Bill Gates, Marc Benioff, and the CEOs of most large technology companies. This book is an amalgamation of business advice that Chris has compiled from his many meetings with successful business people over the past two decades as well as observations of why brilliant entrepreneurs like Steve Jobs or Mark Zuckerberg have become incredibly successful. Business schools do a good job of providing students with theoretical and practical frameworks that can be applicable to real world problems but <u>business schools often miss teaching students some of the most crucial business lessons like how to network or how to find customers or how to get a job!</u>

Chris Haroun has an MBA from Columbia University and a Bachelor of Commerce from McGill University. He is also an award winning MBA university professor at several business schools in the San Francisco Bay Area. He is a frequent guest lecturer and student business model mentor at Berkeley, Stanford and McGill where he is a McGill University Dobson Fellow. Chris also teaches many business courses online at <u>www.Udemy.com/user/chris-haroun</u>. He has work experience at Goldman Sachs, hedge fund giant Citadel, technology consulting firm Accenture, his own start-ups and most recently as a partner at a prominent San Francisco based venture capital firm where he focuses on software and Internet venture capital investments. He is also a frequent guest columnist for Wired Magazine, Venture Beat and Entrepreneur Magazine. He is originally from Canada and resides in Hillsborough, California with his wife and three sons.

Contents

SECTION 1: RELATIONSHIPS ARE MORE IMPORTANT THAN PRODUCT KNOWLEDGE

Crucial Networking Tips to Make You More Successful

LESSON #1: STEVE JOBS' WINNING STRATEGY: HOW TO GET ANYTHING YOU WANT

Many of us use iPhones and iPads and other Apple products because of one simple business and life strategy that Steve Jobs practiced from a very young age:

"Ask and you shall receive." This short YouTube video will change your life (alternatively go to YouTube and search for "Steve Jobs Ask"):
https://www.youtube.com/watch?v=zkTf0LmDqKl

Steve Jobs never had issues reaching out and asking for help from strangers. You will be amazed how many people want to help you if you just ask! Fortunately, not many people do this.

When Steve Jobs was only 12 years old he called Bill Hewlett from Hewlett Packard. The young Steve Jobs asked Bill Hewlett if he could give Steve spare parts for a device that he was creating. Hewlett laughed and not only gave him the spare parts, but gave Steve Jobs a job!

Many of us are too shy or we think that it is outside of our comfort zone to ask for help, especially from strangers. Culturally it feels uncomfortable for many people to ask for help or ask strangers for something. You need to do this often.

So in this day and age of social media, how do we successfully ask for help? It's much easier than you think. If you are not already a LinkedIn subscriber, please sign up for the premium version. Do an advanced search and find people with something in common with you. If you are from Bombay but live in the United States and live in New York, enter Bombay in LinkedIn and then the zip code that you live in. Then send an "inMail" message in LinkedIn with a very short message as follows:

> *John,*
>
> *Hope all is well. I am also from Bombay and I also live in New York. Please let me know if you have time for a coffee in the next few weeks.*
>
> *Thanks a lot,*
> *Chris*

Yes it is that easy! People want to help, especially the farther away you get from the place you grew up in. You can also reach people by leveraging your school as follows:

> *Matt,*
>
> *Hopo all is woll. I also wont to McGill University and I also live in New York. Please let me know if you have time for a coffee in the next few weeks.*
>
> *Thanks a lot,*
> *Chris*

Trust me – this works! My success rate on getting meetings with strangers using LinkedIn has always been very high. Why? Because I ask often and most people don't.

This works exceptionally well. Please try it! It works because very few people do it. Too many people today use email which is why it is not an effective tool to set up meetings.

InMails work. Please try it. I promise you that you will be amazed at the outcome! People want to help you! Simply *ask and you shall receive.*

LESSON #2: HOW TO GET A JOB AND WHY SENDING IN A RESUME CAN BE A WASTE OF TIME...THERE IS A BETTER WAY.

Be a contrarian and think different when it comes to getting a job. Everybody sends their resume to companies. Don't do this as the odds of getting an interview are extraordinarily low.

How do I get a job then? Well it all comes down to the relationships that you already have or will have soon. What does that mean? It's simple as all you need to do is set up informational meetings with as many people as you can at the companies you want to work at.

You are probably asking yourself this question: "That doesn't make any sense. Why would someone want to meet with me anyway and how do I get these meetings?" It is simple. Use LinkedIn. We are covering using LinkedIn several times in this book as it is crucial that you leverage this social media gold mine (because most people don't).

In the business school classes that I teach, I start off every first lecture with a simple question as follows: "If I told you that if you did at least 20 informational meetings with strangers at companies that you wanted to work at then you will get the job of your dreams. If this is the case, how many of you would set up these informational meetings?" Every single student lifts their hand in agreement. Then at the end of the 15 session course that I teach, I ask how many did 20+ informational meetings. Only 1 or 2 hands go up. Those that did the 20+ informational meetings all get jobs without exception.

So are you telling me Chris that if I set up 20 or more informational meetings that I will get a job? That's right. Try it and you'll amaze yourself.

Ok so once I get these meetings what should I do or say? Just be yourself. If the person you are meeting with is from your home town talk about your home town. If this person went to the same school as you did, simply talk about the school. Relationships are more important than product knowledge so the first half of the meeting should be an informal discussion about what you have in common with this person (i.e., the school you went to, where you are from etc.). Then during the second half of the meeting you should transition to a discussion of your career goals. Towards the end of the meeting you need to ask if the company is hiring. If not, ask when they will be and follow up at that point.

This strategy works but you need to meet with many people in order to see the results.

LESSON #3: BUSINESS IS ABOUT PEOPLE AND NOT WHAT YOU KNOW

It's an old cliché that it's not what you know but who you know. If you need to get anything done in your company then you need to develop extraordinary relationships with coworkers in your department and other departments.

In the first few months of starting a new job it's imperative that you grab a coffee or lunch or breakfast with as many people as you can regardless of what level they are at or what departments they work in.

By networking internally at your company you will understand the corporate culture and how to get things done. People want to help you if they like you and feel comfortable speaking with you. These meetings early on are crucial as they are harder to set up once you aren't the new kid in town anymore.

Lesson #4: Treat People Like Celebrities and Celebrities Like People

I recently had dinner with one of President Bush's White House employees in the early 1990s. As I always do when I meet someone successful or that works with someone successful, I ask what makes that person successful. For President Bush, as it is with all successful politicians, it comes down to having superb relationships.

President Bush treats people like celebrities and celebrities like people. Learn as much as you can about people you meet by asking them questions. Let them talk about themselves and smile. Remember their names too. People love talking about themselves and they really appreciate it when you use their name often in conversations.

Treat all people you meet in business like good lifelong friends. Don't jump right into business topics in a conversation. Always start with personal questions like how was your weekend, or do your children like their new school, or something that people love talking about, like their favorite sports teams etc. Treat everyone like they are your friends and treat people like celebrities and celebrities like people.

LESSON #5: MEET PEOPLE, HAVE FUN AND LEARN

Your goal when you start a new job should be to meet people, have fun and learn. Business is about people so develop strong relationships with as many people as you can. If you have a superb network, then you can achieve any goal you want in life as these people are on your team.

Have fun at work too. Be productive but also laugh a lot with friends there. This is crucial as you will likely be spending more time in your life with people at work than you will with your family. Life is too short not to have fun and enjoy the company of those you work with.

Always be learning. Learn from those you work for. Learn from those you work with. Learn from those you don't work with but are in different divisions in your company.

I remember when I was in my 20s and I moved from Canada to New York City to work at Goldman Sachs. I was so nervous. What if they find out that I know nothing compared to my peers? What made the whole experience incredible for me was that I gave myself 3 rudimentary goals when I started working there which was to meet people, have fun and learn.

I set up one meeting each day at Goldman with someone I didn't know. Everyone will take a meeting with you at your company. I met with many partners, associates, vice presidents, managing directors, assistants etc. The most productive meetings were with the assistants as they work with the partners and understand exactly how the firm works. Get to know them well.

LESSON #6: THE IMPORTANCE OF SINCERE GRATITUDE

Thank people often. After an informational interview send a handwritten thank you note. Why? Because almost nobody does this anymore and it is the quintessential personal / straight from the heart act of kindness.

In all of your emails try to use the word please and thank you. This works a heck of a lot better than the cold "Regards" you see at the bottom of many emails. Emails are often misinterpreted as the tone is tough to interpret. As a result, many emails come across as too aggressive even if the intent was a passive message. The solution is to add an element of gratitude in each email.

Here is an example of an email that can be misinterpreted:

> John,
>
> Let's meet at 4pm today.
>
> Regards,
> Chris

This version is much better given the element of gratitude.

> John,
>
> Hope all is well. Let's meet at 4pm today. Please let me know if this works for you.
>
> Thanks,
> Chris

LESSON #7: YOUR ALMA MATTERS

People don't leverage schools that they have attended enough. The friends you make in school are often more beneficial to you and your career than what you actually learned in school! Make sure to leverage your school alumni network often. You will be amazed how many doors are opened using this best practice.

All universities have local alumni sponsored events. If you are not aware of them, call your alumni office and ask them for details on your local alumni club. If one doesn't exist, then here is your golden networking opportunity to start one!

Hewlett Packard was successful because the founders went to school with Disney executives, who signed the first significant contract with Hewlett Packard. There are countless examples of companies that were successful because the founder leveraged her or his alumni network.

Please also use LinkedIn often to leverage your golden alumni network, especially if you live more than a few hundred miles from the school you attended. It's easy to get meetings with alumni using LinkedIn 'inMails'. Simply do an advanced search in LinkedIn and type in the name of the school you attended and the zip or postal code that you live in (or are visiting). Then use this simple format to get meetings:

> John, hope all is well. I am also a graduate of McGill and I will be in Cleveland in May. Please let me know if you have time for a coffee.

Thanks a lot,
Chris

LESSON #8: CRUCIAL POST MEETING NETWORKING BEST PRACTICE

Your success in business is predicated on the strength of your network. After every meeting you have or after every guest speaker that presents to you at a company, school or other event, please add that person to your LinkedIn network.

Many people do background checks on you before meeting or deciding to meet with you. The background check is often done partially using LinkedIn. If you have people in common that you have both met, then your professional credibility rises materially.

I don't recommend adding people to your LinkedIn network that you have not met before as you don't want to dilute this golden networking social media platform.

A networking best practice is that under the person's profile picture in LinkedIn, you can put in a private note that only you can see that identifies how you met and relevant information about the conversation you had with this person.

SECTION 2: BE LONG TERM GREEDY

Use These Crucial Long Term Strategies and Watch Your Net Worth Soar

LESSON #9: THE LONGER THE VIEW THE WISER THE INTENTION

When I worked at Goldman Sachs my mentors would always tell me to "be long term greedy". I didn't fully appreciate it at the time but it makes perfect sense to me now, especially when it comes to investing.

I worked in the hedge fund industry for several years after leaving Goldman Sachs and I hated the industry because investors only rewarded you if you were successful with short term results. The problem with this approach is that you are often right for the wrong reasons and vice versa. Each month has only 20 business or trading days and each quarter has only 60 business or trading days. It is mathematically impossible to generate positive returns every quarter year after year after year.

The best investors have a long term outlook. In fact, before I do due diligence on any company as a potential investment candidate, I ask myself one very basic question:

"In 5 years will this company be more relevant or less relevant than it is today?"

Sounds pretty simple! It should be because the best investors see the forest from the trees and understand that investment trends last much longer than we think. I always ask myself this basic 5 year question before I do any due diligence on companies. Nobody is better at being a wise long term investor than Warren Buffett.

I remember when I was an MBA student at Columbia University in the late 1990s and Warren Buffett was teaching one of our classes on value investing. One of my classmates pitched a technology stock to him. He very politely interrupted 30 seconds after my classmate pitched the stock and said "Son thank you very much for the idea but I don't have enough visibility where this company is going to be product cycle wise in 3, 5, 10 or 20 years."

He was right as 6 months later the technology company my classmate was pitching went belly up; there is a reason Warren Buffett is called the *Sage of Omaha.*

Since I am a proud Canadian, I have to end this chapter with a quote from the greatest athlete ever, the great one (Wayne Gretzky). Gretzky was so incredibly successful because he didn't skate to where the puck is. Rather, he had a longer term strategy as he skated to where the puck was going to be. Love that guy!

Lesson #10: Learn Earn Return

Give and you shall receive. This statement has been true since the beginning of time; those that are generous with their time and mentor others are much more successful than those that are not. Why? First of all it is the right thing to do as others helped you to get to where you are today, but by mentoring others you also reinforce your core beliefs and remind yourself what the drivers of success are.

I am honored to be on the board of a wonderful charity called the LEMO Foundation, whose mission is to eradicate poverty through scholarships to those that are less fortunate. LEMO's core mission statement is brilliant:

"Don't expect to accomplish your goals unless you help others accomplish theirs."

I love this concept! Some call it karma and others call it paying it forward. Everyone should seek mentors and mentor others; you will be much more successful in the long run if you practice what you preach.

LESSON #11: THE HARDER YOU WORK, THE LUCKIER YOU GET

When you first think of an incredibly ambitious goal, you are so fired up and excited to start the journey. Before you start the journey you can clearly see the top of the mountain, which is a metaphor for your goal.

Once you embark upon your journey you are full of energy and excitement as with each step you get closer and closer to your goal. Then much later in the journey you become frustrated as you can no longer see the top of the mountain. As a result, your pace deviates a bit and is perhaps slower than it once was.

You wonder what happened to my goal? Why can't I see the top of the mountain anymore anyway? Well the reason is simple; the reason is that you are half way up the mountain and your goal is within reach. Finish what you started and reap the rewards. Be long term greedy and realize the harder you work, the luckier you get.

LESSON #12: THE MOST IMPORTANT INVESTMENT YOU WILL EVER MAKE

Don't be cheap when it comes to education and self-improvement. You are your biggest investment. Continuous improvement is of paramount importance when it comes to your success in business or life in general.

Spend more than you think you can afford on education, including university degrees, online education, books, audio books, podcasts etc. Whatever it takes. You do have time to read. Yes you do; you can listen to audio books or listen to online lectures. If you have Wi-Fi and a stationary bike at home you can watch online courses at Udemy.com for example.

Be a voracious reader. Read as many books as you can on successful business people. What are their secrets? Learn from them and watch your career take off.

LESSON #13: LEARN WHAT NOT TO DO

You can learn a lot about business by observing your supervisor(s). You can learn a lot by observing what makes them successful and also what their shortfalls are. That's right; learn what not to do.

Observe how your superiors manage people. Observe how their subordinates react to being managed. If your peers have a negative attitude given how they are being treated by their supervisor, then learn what not to do from a management practice as employees that lack passion are not productive.

When I worked in consulting at Accenture in the mid 1990s, I will never forget how poorly I was treated by an associate partner at the firm one night. It was around 10pm and I just started my first job. An associate partner asked me to print out a database report. I had no idea how to do it and I tried hard. I told him that I am very sorry but I can't figure it out. He looked at me and said "it's because you are incompetent." I was shocked at his response and, as a result, I spent several hours a day looking for another job and my morale was crushed.

Had he not reacted that way, I would have been much more proactive and passionate about my role. To be intellectually honest though, I suppose the correct response from me should have been "I don't know but I'll find out".

> *"Good judgement comes from experience.*
> *Experience comes from bad judgement."*

SECTION 3: AVOID BURNOUT

Avoid these Crucial Land Mines and Save your Career (and Your Life)

LESSON #14: WHAT TO DO THE SECOND YOU RETURN FROM VACATION

One of the best pieces of advice I have received in my life was from a client at Manulife Financial when I worked at Goldman Sachs. She told that the second you return from your vacation, open your calendar and look out 6 months and book your next vacation.

Of course I didn't take this advice as I was in my 20s and felt like I had endless energy. Then I hit a wall and became incredibly unproductive. I had worked too many weekends and too many hours per day. In hindsight all I needed to do was take a few weekends off and a whole week every 6 months.

When you work too hard without taking breaks you burnout and become incredibly unproductive. If you work for 3 months, for example, around the clock without many breaks, then I am a firm believer that it will take you more than 3 months to "unburnout". The results can be catastrophic for your career and even your personal life. Pace yourself and take breaks often.

Lesson #15: Stress Will Kill You; Don't be the Gazelle!

As humans we are only supposed to be incredibly stressed out when we are fighting for our lives. We were not meant to have heart attacks because of non-violent means.

When a lion is chasing a gazelle, the gazelle's physiology dramatically changes. The gazelle's heart is pumping very fast as it runs as fast as it can to survive. The gazelle's body uses every ounce of energy to focus on surviving. Other bodily functions temporarily cease working as it tries to outrun the lion. The gazelle's immune system shuts down. The gazelle's reproductive system shuts down. The gazelle actually ages in the process.

Similarly, when we feel too much stress at work and don't treat our systems the way we should, we get sick much easier, we gain weight much faster, our heart can stop working and even our reproductive capacities are adversely impacted.

I have several friends that couldn't seem to conceive. As a couple they became so incredibly stressed out with their perceived conceiving issues that they stopped trying and adopted wonderful children. Shortly after adoption, they had no problems conceiving because they were no longer stressed out.

Stress will kill you; don't be the gazelle. See stress as a challenge and not as a threat. Learn to take breaks. Don't walk into the propeller. Hakuna matata! :)

Lesson #16: When to Take a Day Off When You are Not Sick

We tend to take sick days because we are physically under the weather. We need to also take at least one day off per year when we are temporarily 'mentally under the weather'. This is usually caused by overexertion and not taking enough breaks.

Why should we take that day off? Because if you are too stressed out, you might have a short temper and upset your coworkers or customers. If you are overly stressed, take a day off. Your career will thank you and remember to pace yourself and take breaks often enough so that you don't need to miss work too often.

Lesson #17: The Ten Commandments

In several religions, one of the ten rules is to rest on the 7th day. Our ancestors knew about burnout thousands of years ago! You need to take off at least one day per week.

Since my 30s I have not allowed myself to check my work email on Sundays. In fact, I have taught my kids to give me crap if I work on Sunday. They are helping me to not get burned out. Family always comes first, especially on Sundays for me.

Hopefully your partners, supervisors or clients all have children and spend time with their families on the weekend instead of working. If not, you should very politely and politically let them know that your family comes first on weekends (especially Sunday). Heck you come first on Sundays too; relax and recover. You deserve it!

Section 4: Create Off the Charts Confidence; Wear that Superman Cape!

Crucial Confidence Lessons to Help Your Career Take Off!

LESSON #18: THERE ARE NO LIMITS

Whether or not you think you can, you are correct. You need to accept the fact that if you want to be the CEO of the company you are working at, it's not hard to do unless you tell yourself it is. It doesn't matter what level you are at either as there are countless examples of people that have started in the mail room and then risen to become CEO. Don't be negative. I promise you that you can become the CEO regardless of your education or rank at the company.

Similarly, you can start any company you want to and disrupt an entire industry regardless of your education. Bill Gates, Mark Zuckerberg and Steve Jobs don't have university degrees. What they have is an unquenchable thirst to leave a dent in the universe. Believe in yourself and you can accomplish any goals you want to in business.

We can sometimes overestimate what we can accomplish in a year but we ALWAYS massively underestimate what we can accomplish in a decade. There are no limits to what you can achieve in business except the ones that you personally set. Whether or not you think you can, you are correct (that was worth repeating).

Lesson #19: The Glass is Always Full

In every challenging business situation, it is imperative that you see challenge as an opportunity. I am a firm believer that with crisis comes opportunity. Rise to the occasion when a crisis emerges

Condition yourself to embrace change and enjoy difficult situations. This will help you deal with the perceived stress and profit from adversity. Always ask yourself in business "what is positive about this event and how can I enjoy and benefit from it?" If you hate an uncompromising situation or position you are in, meditate on the issue and condition yourself to accept the fact that the end result from this situation will be very positive for you if you achieve 'X'. Focus on X and make it come to reality.

The belief that anything is possible leads to amazing accomplishments.

The glass is not empty.

The glass not half empty.

The glass is not half full.

The glass is **ALWAYS** full!

LESSON #20: BALANCED LIFE = MORE PRODUCTIVE IN BUSINESS

You have time to do anything every day. That's right. Learn time management practices. Before you go to bed, make tomorrow's calendar and make sure it includes time with family/friends, time for exercise, time for choosing/eating the right food, time for sleep and yes time for work.

You always have time for people. You always have time to exercise. You always have time for family and friends. You always have time for rest. Telling yourself that you don't have time is just a result of poor time management. As you get older and especially when you have children, you will learn to only focus on the most important drivers of your life. Please remember to put together tomorrow's calendar today.

I make time to exercise every single day and I am much more productive because of this. When you exercise, it releases serotonin and keeps you having a positive attitude and makes you much more productive.

I find that when I take long vacations, although I have fun, I am incredibly unproductive. The busier you are, the more you can accomplish in all aspects of your life. Have a balanced life. Don't procrastinate. Always tell yourself when you have a task at hand this: "I do it now. I do it now. I do it now." Life is too short to put things off. Let's turn a perceived weakness into a strength!

LESSON #21: YOU ARE NEVER AS NERVOUS AS YOU SOUND

At times when we meet with senior executives or make presentations, we feel nervous. Don't worry because 99% of the time you are never as nervous as you sound! This should put you at ease. In fact, when you condition yourself to enjoy presenting or meeting with senior executives, you of course don't sound nervous, and you don't feel nervous at all!

Keep in mind that when you give presentations you always know more about the presentation topic than anyone in the audience. You only feel nervous because you tell yourself you are nervous. Just be yourself and tell yourself that you really enjoy the company of the audience; pretend they are your life-long friends and family members and they love you and want nothing more than for you to be extremely successful.

If you feel nervous just think of a time when you were extremely successful and get yourself in that exact state of mind. Going forward, look forward to perceived uncomfortable situations where you have felt nervous in the past; enjoy these moments and see them as challenges as your competitors won't.

Lesson #22: Avoid "Those" People

Don't let the bastards get you down. That's right. If you can, going forward disassociate yourself with negative people. Friends with negative attitudes are not worth having. Surround yourself with positive people that believe there are no limits to what they and you can achieve. Surround yourself with people that are incredibly successful as their success, confidence and positive outlook on business and life will rub off on you and vice versa.

Surround yourself with positive people and the chances of you being extraordinarily successful rises 1,000,000%. I have never met a successful entrepreneur, investor or CEO that doesn't have a positive attitude. Richard Branson is the quintessential example of a positive role model. I believe that his cheerful and positive outlook in life and business is the primary reason for his incredible success. His positive attitude is the cornerstone of the happy and positive corporate culture at all of his Virgin companies. Try flying Virgin America or Virgin Atlantic or one day Virgin Galactic and observe how amazing the attitude is of all of his employees. A company with an incredibly positive corporate culture will no doubt be much more successful than a company filled with negative people. A negative person would never consider launching a galactic service or taking on the airline industry. Richard Branson clearly avoids hiring "those" people.

LESSON #23: THAT PERSON SPEAKS "GOODER" THAN ME!

Don't get fooled by assuming that someone in business is smarter than you because they speak "gooder" than you. They might be born with a silver spoon in their mouth and they might have gotten in to Harvard Business School (HBS) because one of their relatives went there. Remember that two thirds of HBS is BS! ;)   Just kidding (sort of)...always remember that you earned your way to where you are today and the fact that some people speak more eloquently than you do is not a reflection of them having higher intelligence. "Au contraire"; they are likely more insecure than you are. Unfortunately in business, confidence leads to perceived competence.

LESSON #24: NOBODY IS SMARTER THAN YOU

Please accept that fact that everything around you in business was created by people that are no smarter than you. I am not asking you to be arrogant. Rather, I am asking you to materially increase your confidence but accepting the fact that you are the smartest person in the world.

Why am I making such an outrageous request? Because if you believe it then you can accomplish any goal that you create in life regardless of how unrealistic others think it is. Actually, who cares what others think anyway!

Quite often the reason people are not successful in business is because they are insecure and believe that they are not smart enough to accomplish their goals.

Please watch this short YouTube video by Steve Jobs as it will change your life (or search on YouTube for "Steve Jobs Smarter than You"):
https://www.youtube.com/watch?v=UvEiSa6_EPA

SECTION 5: ETHICS. USE IT OR LOSE IT

Crucial Ethics Lessons to Keep You Out of Trouble

Lesson #25: Transparency Builds Trust

Always be 100% transparent in business, especially with the risks of the product or service you are selling. I tell my investors and customers what the risks are of investing in my products or services within 5 minutes of our first meeting. It's the right and ethical thing to do. It also leads to trust which is of paramount importance in business.

Disclose all risks to your clients or prospective clients before doing business with them. To state the obvious, they will be incredibly upset if you don't as they will always find out the risks at some point, which could result in painful litigation. The only reason you might not offer 100% disclosure is in the rare situation when you can't divulge an issue due to confidentiality reasons. If this is the case and if the investment or product/service has significant risks that outweigh the potential returns, then don't sell the product/service. Life is too short to destroy your reputation and compromise your values.

Lesson #26: Don't Trust this Type of Person

I will never do business with someone that cheats on their spouse. If their closest confidant and spouse can't trust them then neither can I.

A businessperson that is unethical just one time is likely to be unethical again, again and again. Before hiring someone or accepting a job offer or working with a business partner, make sure to leverage LinkedIn and do as many background checks as you can to make sure this person is ethical.

I have found that the older I get when I do background checks, the less likely people are to say negative things especially in writing. As a result, when you speak with people when doing background checks, you can read their body language and if they don't have very positive things to say about someone, then interpret this as a negative; where there is smoke there is fire.

Other people in business that I don't trust are those that backstab others (outside of doing background checks). Chances are if they are bad mouthing others, they will do the same to you.

Watch your back around these types of people.

LESSON #27: HOW TO TELL IF SOMEONE IS LYING

When I worked at a large hedge fund called Citadel, management hired 25 year CIA and FBI veterans to teach us how to tell if a CEO is lying to us. Here are some of the key takeaways:

1: A liar often gives long winded answers to a simple yes or no question.

2: A liar often does not make eye contact when answering a question and the answer contains a lie (unless this is their normal demeanor).

3: A liar often puts their hand on their mouth when answering a question with a lie.

4: A liar often shakes his or her foot when answering a question with a lie (unless they drink too much coffee)!

LESSON #28: HOW TO DESTROY YOUR CAREER IN 30 SECONDS OR LESS

The only thing you bring with you from one company to the next is your reputation; that's all you have and nothing is more important! Warren Buffett famously said that it takes 30 years to build a reputation and 30 seconds to ruin it!

Be especially careful with electronic messages and social media. Always assume that whatever you write on your computer/tablet/smartphone will be stored forever and can be accessed by anyone. The same can unfortunately be said for voicemail.

I remember my first day of work at Goldman Sachs. On the first day the company welcomed all of us I my start class, then they fingerprinted us and said "Welcome to Goldman Sachs, you have the ability to do more harm than good at this firm; don't ever do anything that can get you or the firm's name on the cover of the Wall Street Journal." I have always admired Goldman's long term greedy and ethical business practices.

SECTION 6: EVERY BATTLE IS WON BEFORE IT HAS BEEN FOUGHT

Crucial Battle Preparation Lessons

LESSON #29: OVER PREPARE FOR EVERYTHING

Always over prepare, especially for job interviews. If your competition likely only spends 5 hours preparing for a meeting then spend 50 hours preparing. If your competition spends 10 hours preparing for a meeting, spend 100 hours.

Every battle is won before it has been fought. Be ready. Bring many exhibits to meetings and leave them in your briefcase. Pull them out of your briefcase if you need to show them as exhibits. I have done this many times in interviews and have often gotten hired because of this. Anticipate what questions the interviewer asks you before the interview.

When I had my interviews for MBA school and at Goldman Sachs, I completely over prepared. I wrote down over 100 questions that I thought they might ask me and then I recorded myself answering the questions. Did my voice sound too monotone? Did I sound over confident? Did I sound nervous (no way)? Were my answers short enough? Did my answers sound interested and engaging? Etc.

A friend of mine at Stanford was one of the early venture capital investors in Facebook. Of course I asked her why she was successful in winning the investment mandate in Facebook. Her response was that she over prepared for the meeting with Mark Zuckerberg. She brought 3 term sheets (contracts) to the meeting with 3 different dollar values and terms. She gauged his level of criteria for the investment mandate and was able to pull out the term sheet with the terms that Zuckerberg was asking for. Her competition only brought 1 term sheet each. As a result, she won the investment mandate and made a fortune.

Lesson #30: The O'Hare Test - Pass it and Watch Your Career Take Off

Chicago's O'Hare airport is one of the largest airports in the world. The "O'Hare Test" is a personality test that you must pass in order to get hired, promoted and be a superb salesperson.

What is the O'Hare Test and why does it matter in business? The O'Hare test is this: if you are stranded at an airport for 8 hours between flights, can you tolerate and enjoy the company of the colleague stranded with you!

Do they enjoy your company?

Do you spend more time listening than talking?

Do you ask them more questions about themselves and watch them enjoy telling you their life story?

Do they trust you?

If the answers to the 4 questions above are yes, then congratulations, you passed the O'Hare Test! When you interview at a company or meet with a potential customer or conduct an informational interview, the first half of the initial meeting should be conducted like it is the O'Hare Test.

LESSON #31: NEVER TAKE A SHORTCUT YOU HAVE NEVER TAKEN BEFORE WHEN YOU ARE IN A HURRY

How often has this scenario happened to you: you are late for a meeting so you take a shortcut that you have never taken before. As a result, you end up taking longer to get to the meeting than if you had taken the route you had initially planned to take! Simply leave earlier and get to all meetings at least 15 minutes before they start. This will lead to business partners, customers, colleagues and supervisors assuming that you are reliable, which leads to career advancement in the long run.

The same can be said for deadlines. Be careful when cutting corners in order to meet a deadline. Don't ever sacrifice the quality of your work. Always have a contingency plan in place and always plan to deliver your deliverables well ahead of schedule.

SECTION 7: GOAL SETTING

*Follow these **Crucial** Steps and Achieve Your Dreams*

LESSON #32: RUN TO YOUR FEARS

If something scared the heck out of you in business, chances are it also scares your competition. As a result, run to your fears. Don't get too comfortable in life. Always challenge yourself and focus on continuous improvement.

When I was younger I was terrified of public speaking. This fear was holding me back and stopping me from growing professionally. I then did something radically different and incredibly uncomfortable. I thought how can I challenge myself to conquer this fear while helping people? I decided to volunteer with my church and go into the prison system here in the Bay Area and help mentor inmates that were incarcerated for minor drug offenses. I don't do drugs but I feel bad for these young people that didn't have parents or positive role models growing up and, as a result, committed a minor crime and are in jail; this could have been me had I not had two wonderful parents raising me.

I remember the first day I went into the Maguire Correctional facility in Redwood City. I was terrified while presenting to a just a few inmates. I remember one of them had a tattoo above his upper lip that said #&@# you! I thought WTF, which means why the face :) and how the heck am I going to get through this? It was uncomfortable the first time, but I came back again and again and again and I got used to it.

The seminal moment that helped me to conquer my fear of public speaking was the time I showed up at the prison on a Sunday and the priest that was supposed to conduct mass and give the speech before communion didn't show up! I was told by the warden that I must be the Eucharistic minister and give a 20 minute speech to the inmates. I was so terrified. The speech according to the Gospel lesson was supposed to be about faith, hope and confidence in yourself. I stood up there in front of many incredibly intimidating inmates and started speaking. I was able to wing it and a few minutes later I started enjoying it! I will never forget this moment as I told them this: "Do you believe in God?" They all said yes. I then said "Does God believe in you?" The all said yes. I then closed the circular logic by saying "Well if you don't believe in yourself then do you really believe in….?" They were blown away and speechless as was I.

I was able to conquer my fear of public speaking forever and I now thrive and really look forward to public speaking and being on panels. Who knew that my biggest fear in life would become my biggest source of enjoyment! Please run towards your business fears as your competition will not.

We need to change the lens for which we see the world.

:)

Lesson #33: Make a Gap Analysis

Think of the most ambitious goal you can achieve in your life. Don't ask yourself if it is achievable; of course it is. Rather, ask yourself what you need to accomplish in order to make this goal a reality.

Make a rudimentary gap analysis. Once you know what your goal is then focus on the gap, meaning what you need to accomplish in order to make this goal a reality.

I recently met with a former army officer who shared with me declassified information on how to decrease road side bombs from detonating overseas. Army officials were brainstorming on how to make operations safer for them overseas. They couldn't reduce the number of roadside bombs unless they built a mobile data center, which sounded ludicrous and unrealistic. In order to build a mobile data center there was a material gap that they needed to fill, including deploying many engineers, hardware, software, mobile products etc. They ended up filling this gap and so can you in business. I guarantee you that your gap analysis will be more achievable than the one that the army filled.

Set a goal so big that you can't achieve it until you become the person that actually can achieve it.

LESSON #34: YALE UNIVERSITY'S FASCINATING GOAL SETTING STUDY

You need to write down your business goals. If you do, the chances of you realizing them rises materially and most of your competitors don't do this anyway.

In 1953 there was a famous study conducted at Yale University. The graduating class was asked if they had written down their goals. Only 3% had done so. Then 20 years later, a poll was taken and the graduating students from the class of 1953 were asked what their net worth was. The net worth of the 3% that had written down their goals was greater than the other 97% combined!

Write down your goals on the back of a business card and carry it around with you. If you don't carry a wallet, then write down your goals in your smart phone's calendar and have this calendar entry be repeated daily.

Tell your friends or family members what your long term goals are so that it forces you to work towards them and think of your goals often. Consider writing your goals down on paper and then placing them in a sealed and stamped envelope with your address on the envelope. Then give the envelope to a good friend or family member and tell them to mail the letter in 6 months or 1 year.

LESSON #35: SHOULD YOU GET A GRADUATE DEGREE?

Many readers of this book have undergraduate degrees that might have covered many business topics. Should you bother getting a graduate business or law or engineering or other degrees? Only if you need another degree in order to change careers. Only if getting a graduate degree will likely get you closer to your goals.

Do I need to get the best grades and standardized test scores to get into a great school? Heck no! Please go to www.udemy.com and search for my name (Chris Haroun). Take my course on getting into the top MBA schools for tips on how to get in.

LESSON #36: PUSH THE GOAL POST OUT

You need to always be growing professionally. Once your goals are within your reach, it is imperative (after you celebrate your success) to set new almost unachievable goals. Keep challenging yourself. Keep asking yourself for more. Never underestimate the power of a positive attitude. There is no reason you can't be CEO or can't start a company or can't reinvent an industry or can't make a fortune and start the most bad ass charity. The only obstacle standing in your way is you!

SECTION 8: HAPPINESS IS...

[It is Crucial that you] "Find an Occupation You Love and You'll Never Work a Day in Your Life.'

-Confucius.

Lesson #37: Don't Have Job. Instead Have a Passion. Be Happy and Achieve All Your Business Goals.

Success does not lead to happiness; happiness, leads to success. I often tell my students that if they "have a job then they are doing it wrong". Instead, it's tremendously important to "have a passion".

Don't worry about money early in your career; if you follow your passion, then everything else will fall into place. Many of my students want to become an investment banker but then they hate it and are miserable once they start. Focus on what you love doing most in life. The best entrepreneurs don't have a job; they have a passion. Superb examples of passionate entrepreneurs include Sir Richard Branson of Virgin, Mark Benioff of Salesforce, Christian Chabot of Tableau and of course Steve Jobs. The best CEOs and businesspeople in the world are passionate salespeople.

LESSON #38: LAUGH AT YOUR FAILURES

Laugh at your failures and shortfalls and you will enjoy your profession and live a much longer happier life! Self-deprecation is an admirable trait. Find humor in all stressful situations. This instantly changes your state and will help you to focus on turning a crisis into an opportunity.

Comedy is often a result of tragedy plus time. With your business career truncate the time and find humor in your shortcomings immediately. Rather than be depressed given a perceived failure, smile and cheer up because your future incredible success in business is a result of that failure. You will be grateful later in life that you"failed".

There are so many amazing examples of executives that have failed or have been fired which forced them to realize their dreams by starting their own company. Frustration often leads to breakthroughs in your career.

Here are some incredibly inspirational examples of people that were fired. Thank goodness they were or we wouldn't enjoy the benefits of their future business empire creations:

1. Tomas Edison was fired by Western Union.
2. Michael Bloomberg was fired which made him get his revenge by starting his financial empire Bloomberg. Without getting fired he wouldn't have ever become the Mayor of New York.
3. J.K Rowling hated her job as an administrative assistant. She quit and found her passion, which was writing the Harry Potter books.
4. Walt Disney was fired by a publication he worked for.
5. Madonna was fired from Dunkin Donuts

6. Robert Redford was fired from an oil company.
7. Lee Iacocca was fired from Ford. So he turned around and led Chrysler.

<u>All these amazing people lost their jobs because of a lack of passion for being someone else's bitch</u> (sorry about the strong language but I want to make a point). They then became incredibly successful because they focused on their passion.

Find out what your passion is and what you were put on this planet to do. What is your calling? What is your raison d'être? Find your passion and you will always be happy in business and in life. If you feel suffocated in your current job, then find your passion, write a business plan and quit.

LESSON #39: MONEY DOES NOT = HAPPINESS

When I started my second company, I was stressed out and I took a drive alone down the beautiful California coast. I stopped by Carmel and I went for a long walk as I often do to come up with personal and professional goals. I stopped by a beautiful old church and I sat down and collected my thoughts.

A priest was there and sat down next to me. We spoke for a while about what I was trying to accomplish in life. I mentioned that I wanted to make as much money as possible so that I could give my children the standard of living that I wanted them to have. What he told me that day was incredibly prophetic and just what I needed to hear:

"Chris, 50 years from now your children will not look back on you and remember how much money you made. They will look back and reflect how good of a father you were."

I was blown away by his comment and I thanked him profusely for imparting this incredible wisdom on me. I now know in my heart that money does not equal happiness. Please don't make it your primary goal. Find your passion in life and the money will come whether you want it to or not! Then you can focus on giving it away and making the world a better place.

I have seen money destroy friendships and families so many times. Money can destroy your relationship with many people including your children. Give most of your money away to charities and only keep enough to keep your family happy as counterintuitive as that might sound.

LESSON #40: PERSONAL GRATITUDE AND HAPPINESS

You will be much more successful in business if you have sincere personal gratitude for what you have. Years ago I read *The Art of Happiness* by the Dalai Lama. He said that in western society people are so unhappy as we tend to compare ourselves to those that have more than us. By contrast, those that live in second, or third world countries are happier than we are as they focus on what is important in life, like family and friends and a beautiful day!

If we are grateful for at least one different thing in our lives every day and help others that are less fortunate, then we will all lead more fulfilled lives. At night when I say prayers with my 3 wonderful children, I always make them thank God for something different every day.

If we spend more time helping others that are less fortunate, we will all be much more fulfilled and we will be much for successful in life.

So how is this relevant in a book on business? It is incredibly relevant because we will be much more productive in business if we are fulfilled, grateful and happy personally.

Lesson #41: All Your Wealth Can't Buy You Health

If you are happy in your life personally and professionally, then you will be much more productive. You need to find time to exercise daily (no excuses) and focus on nutrition (no excuses) and getting 7-8 hours of sleep per night (no excuses).

Here is another simple rule to stay happy at work: stand up and work while standing for half of the day. I promise you that your productivity and level of happiness will increase materially if you stand often at work and exercise daily. Nothing is more important. Exercising daily helps you think more clearly and be generally happier at work. That positive attitude will remain elevated with exercise.

The Dalai Lama, when asked what surprised him most about humanity, answered:

"Man. Because he sacrifices his health in order to make money. Then he sacrifices money to recuperate health. And then he is so anxious about the future that he does not enjoy the present; the result being that he does not live in the present or the future; he lives as if he is never going to die, and then dies having never really lived."

LESSON #42: WHEN TO CHANGE CAREERS

If you get up in the morning and tell yourself that you are going to work then you are doing it wrong. If you have a job then you are doing it wrong. You need to have a passion. Find out what you are most passionate about in life and make that what you do daily.

I have changed careers several times in my life. I have been fortunate enough to have embraced networking from a young age. I started out in the technology consulting business. I then changed careers post my MBA and worked on Wall Street at Goldman Sachs. I loved the people there but I also understood why so many successful politicians come out of Goldman. So I switched careers and worked in the hedge fund industry because I wanted to make a lot of money. I did ok but I was miserable. Don't work because you want to make a lot of money! I hated the hedge fund industry because it was so short term focused. I wanted to be a long term investor so I started a firm that invested partially in private companies and I ended up getting a great gig as a partner at a prominent Bay Area venture capital firm. I love my business partners. They love what they do as well. They are wonderful family oriented people too. They have their priorities straight (family first). I am also a professor at night. I love helping students and I love sitting on boards and helping companies too. It took me many years to find happiness in what I do and it certainly is not because of the money.....it never is and it never will be.

SECTION 9: LEGAL STUFF IS IMPORTANT

Crucial Lessons on Protecting Your Family and Yourself

Lesson #43: How to Protect Your Family

When you start a company you need to protect your family. Don't set your company up as a sole proprietorship. Rather, set it up as a Limited Liability Company (LLC). Setting up an LLC is not expensive and if for some crazy reason your company gets sued, then the liabilities are limited to the assets of the company and not your house.

If you are working for someone else, you need to have a contract that clearly outlines your compensation structure in case you get hit by a bus. This way your family is taken care of.

I know that this sounds like common sense, but sometimes we are so focused on building our careers and our companies that we forget about protecting those that we love.

LESSON #44: SEEK HELP FROM OUTSIDE COUNSEL

Your business partners or your employer has a lawyer to draft your employment contract. Your employer is most definitely well intentioned and loves you otherwise you wouldn't have the job. However, your employer's lawyer has different intentions and you need to understand this.

Your employer's lawyer(s) always drafts legal documents to protect their client and not you. What can you do about this? Well you can hire your own lawyer to take a look at the documents that your employer's lawyer (not your employer) drafted and make modifications to protect you and your family. It's not personal, it's business and your employer will understand and should be cool with the fact that you want to protect your family.

LESSON #45: STAY OUT OF TROUBLE

It goes without saying that you should be extremely careful with email, electronic forms of communication and voicemail. But you also need to be very careful with dating in the workplace unless you are confident that this person that you are dating is your soulmate.

Interoffice dating can be incredibly distracting for you and for your colleagues. I have seen several occasions where at least one of the people in a relationship at work ended up losing their job. It's not worth it.

SECTION 10: MANAGEMENT BEST PRACTICES

The Most Crucial Business Revelation is that Ideas are Commodities. Execution is Not.

LESSON #46: PRAISE IN PUBLIC AND CRITICIZE IN PRIVATE

Most managers don't offer enough positive feedback to employees and most managers take the wrong approach when criticizing employees.

There is a CEO named Godfrey Sullivan of a very successful Silicon Valley company called Splunk. One of the many reasons the company has seen torrid growth over the past few years is because of the superb management style of Mr. Sullivan. His genius is that he always praises his employees in public and when he needs to offer constructive criticism he does this in private and one on one. This has led to the creation of one of the best corporate cultures in the history of the software sector.

LESSON #47: BE UNEMOTIONAL IN BUSINESS

The most successful portfolio managers on Wall Street and the most successful C level executives and politicians are relatively unemotional. It is very rare for a president or prime minister to ever show public forms of being too emotional.

In business, I have found that successful executives oddly enough never get too happy when things go well and they are never too unhappy when things go poorly. This is especially true of successful money managers. Successful business executives make decisions with a clear mind and don't let their emotions get the best of them.

Observe your feelings; do not become them.

Lesson #48: What is the Most Important Investment Characteristic?

Ideas are commodities but execution is not. Business executives and money managers often make the mistake of focusing too much attention on evaluating a business model and not enough time ensuring that the best managers are running the business.

This is especially true in the money management or venture capital sector where the most important success factor in any investment is making sure that you have the right management team in place.

Past performance <u>is</u> indicative of future performance if you have the right CEO and right management team. Yes that was a very controversial statement but I believe that if you bet on a management team that has been extraordinarily successful in the past, then your chance of success betting on this management team in the future is materially higher than betting against a B or C management team.

Always bet on the jockey and not on the horse.

LESSON #49: HIRE SLOWLY AND FIRE QUICKLY

Take as much time as you can figuring out who to hire. Obviously make sure they are qualified. Make sure that they fit in with your corporate culture. Make sure that they are team players. Make sure that each of your employees that will work with the person you are hiring meets with them at least 3 times and in different settings (i.e., your office, then a coffee shop and then a restaurant).

It's important that you don't ask for references as this process is ridiculous. Who in the world would give references for people that will say bad stuff about them anyway! Rather, find your own references, which includes companies the candidate has worked at before or contacts that you have in common with the candidate in LinkedIn etc.

You need to fire quickly. If you let a disgruntled employee stick around for too long then, then he or she will destroy your corporate culture; a small leak can sink a great ship.

The best way to let somebody go is to sit down with them and start by giving them a genuine compliment on their accomplishments. Then tell them that they are being let go in 2 sentences or less and the reason(s) why. Then pause to see what their reaction is. Less is more. You don't need to sound apologetic at all. The first time you let someone go is always the hardest but it gets a lot easier (unfortunately). If necessary, have a security guard be present if the employee seems incredibly erratic, which is rare. Quite often you will be helping this person out in the long run (please see the section titled Laugh at Your Failures).

A colleague of mine on Wall Street once told me that "you're not a real person until you have been fired!" It has happened to me before despite the fact that I made the firm a lot of money. Unfortunately resentment from your boss can be an issue if you do your job too well! If that's the case, start your own company. When it happened to me I gave him a hug and remained incredibly professional as I knew that he would be a reference for my next gig. Remember to always be unemotional about business and be long term greedy. It was actually the best thing that ever happened to me in business as it forced me to focus on my passion and not work.

LESSON #50: TOUCH HAND ONLY ONCE

Learn to deal with issues quickly and only once. In the old days before email we would receive paper memos on our desk. The best practice then was to deal with a memo immediately and only let it touch your hand once before placing it in your physical outbox on your desk. The same should be said for emails, messages, texts etc. The second you see them, deal with them immediately. If the task will take more than a few minutes then flag them and follow up with them later in the day. I know that this process sounds overly simplistic, but you can save a lot of time by not procrastinating and dealing will all minor tasks as they arrive. Keep saying to yourself: "I do it now. I do it now. I do it now!"

SECTION 11: NAVIGATING CORPORATE POLITICS; SWIMMING WITH SHARKS.

Crucial Lessons on Navigating Corporate Politics

LESSON #51: KEEP THAT LETTER IN YOUR DRAWER

My father used to tell me that if he is ever upset and writes a critical letter (which is rare for him), then don't mail it that day. Rather, put it in your drawer before you go to sleep. When you wake up the next morning, if you still feel like mailing the letter then get it from the drawer and drop it in the post.

The same strategy should be used today. If you are in a bad mood or if you are not sure if your tone will be misunderstood when composing an email or a text, then save it as a draft or consider sending it the following day when you are in a different state of mind. It is so easy to hurt your career if you react on impulse with messages and you aren't thinking clearly; one misread or mistaken message can ruin your career; we live in interesting digital times.

LESSON #52: RELIGION AND POLITICS

Most of us know that this one is common sense but it is worth discussing briefly. If half a country votes for X candidate and the other half votes for Y candidate then disclosing your political preference might piss off 50% of your peers. So don't talk about politics and don't put your political affiliation online or on your LinkedIn profile. Many people do this by 'following' politicians on LinkedIn or on Twitter. It's not worth it. It's questionable if you should even ever make political donations as they are publically disclosed online. I suppose this is a reason why some people give to both parties!

Lesson #53: Unjustified Criticism is a Disguised Compliment

I used to get sensitive and upset when others would criticize or insult me. I don't let this bother me anymore. In fact the more successful in life you get, the more this will happen to you. How should you react? Well first of all I hope this happens to you more often because it is a reflection of your success. You want this to happen more often as it is incredibly flattering. Your coworkers might develop a more condescending tone with you over the years the more successful you become as well. You almost want to reach out and thank them for the disguised complement! Don't worry because they just feel threatened by you which is a euphemism for a huge compliment.

Successful people are criticized all the time. The ones that are the happiest and have the best peace of mind are those that see criticism as nothing more than a disguised complement. So bring it on doubters! :)

LESSON #54: HOW TO TALK BEHIND PEOPLE'S BACKS

Here is a recipe for the only way to talk behind people's backs: ONLY SAY NICE THINGS! If you have nothing nice to say, then say nothing at all. There is absolutely no upside in criticizing or condemning or complaining.

If you complain behind other's backs, people will not trust you as they will expect you to do the same to them. This isn't high school.

Don't criticize your co-workers at home either. What is the upside of that? It will destroy your morale, your productivity and your happiness. It's also bad karma. Mean people suck.

LESSON #55: OBSERVE THEN MAKE YOUR MOVE

Every firm has a radically different corporate culture. Stuff gets done in different ways in different firms. When you join a new company it's important to take time to understand how decisions get made and who can help you make these decisions. I know this might sound elusive but please keep in mind that all corporate cultures are different.

In some corporate cultures being a type A personality and very aggressive will help you advance. In other corporate cultures being the quintessential team player with a type B personality works best. If you are too aggressive at a firm with a more gentle or passive corporate culture then you might be hurting your career by being too aggressive and vice versa.

There is even a subtle email and communication corporate culture in each company that is completely unique compared to other companies. You need to learn how to navigate communication protocols of different corporate cultures.

Think of a company's corporate culture as being commensurate with the culture of a country you are visiting for the first time. You don't want to offend anyone when you visit a new country and are unclear what the corporate culture is like there. For example, I used to work in Japan and I had to read a book on Japanese business culture before starting work. Had I not observed Japanese business cross cultural differences, then I would have given customers in Japan my business card with one hand instead of two hands and I would have not known that patting colleagues on the back is not acceptable.

Lesson #56: The Army Promotes You Because of This

We have all seen movies where the Sargent yells at her or his subordinates. The subordinates have to suck it up and take it or they can't get promoted. They deal with the verbal abuse for ages until they earn the right to advance to the next level.

I know that this section seems extreme but I am trying to make a subtle point. You need to deal with respecting the management style of your supervisor no matter what (within reason) in order to get promoted. Similar to the section on corporate culture, each manager and company and department has their own subtle management practices that you must respect in order to make it to the next level. Turn the other cheek and keep your eyes on the prize.

For those of you that hate this chapter (and I hope most of you do as I cringed while writing it), then channel this frustration into writing a business plan on how to launch your own company. Please see www.udemy.com and search for my name (Chris Haroun) to find courses that can help you to start a new company.

With frustration comes breakthrough.

LESSON #57: WHY FACE TIME IS IMPORTANT (UGH)

Until you start your own company, I hate to say it but face time is important, especially when you start a new job.

In accounting there is an inventory term called FIFO, which stands for First In First Out. There is also another accounting inventory term called LIFO, which stands for Last In First Out. I coined a term early in my career called FILO, which stands for First In Last Out. When you start your first full-time job you need to show up to work before anyone and leave work after everyone. This will ensure that the people that decide on who gets promoted understand that you have an incredibly dedicated work ethic.

I really cringed when I wrote this chapter but I think it is important especially when you are new to an industry and are trying to make a great first impression. If this chapter frustrates you (and I hope it does), then please channel your frustration into writing a kick ass business plan and starting your own company. It is worth repeating: with frustration comes breakthrough.

LESSON #58: D.T.A. | SHARKS ARE TOUGH TO SPOT SOMETIMES

D.T.A stands for "Don't Trust Anyone". Sharks are not always easy to spot in a corporate culture. Many aggressive type A sharks are easy to spot, but there are also more passive sharks that like to think they keep their friends close and their enemies closer. I am not a cynical guy at all but I have seen many sharks in my career and you need to be careful around them as they believe that your failure leads to their success. They are insecure too as they want you to fail.

Some sharks are tough to spot. You can tell who they are in the way that they ask questions. Their tone might be very slightly condescending. If so, watch out! Other ways to tell who the sharks are is their subtle reaction to one of your achievements.

So what do you do around them? Just keep your cards close to your chest and have a positive attitude. Don't ever tell them anything that you don't want repeated. Assume every word you tell these sharks can be broadcast to everyone in your company. D.T.A.

LESSON #59: A VALUABLE LESSON ABOUT DONALD TRUMP

Regardless of your political views, Donald Trump is right about this: "If you don't tell people about your successes, they will never know."

I was raised to be incredibly humble in Canada and I am very proud of my upbringing and my heritage. However, you need to find ways to remind your boss or your clients or potential recruiters about your success. Nobody will brag about you. Nobody will help you advance. You need to help yourself. If you don't feel comfortable doing this then ask people to write positive reviews for you on LinkedIn.

There are so many other great quotes for this section from sports, including "You are only as good as your last game." People have an incredibly short attention span. If you don't remind them of your accomplishments, then it's game over for your career.

LESSON #60: ASK "HOW AM I DOING?" OFTEN

I have had many friends in the companies that I have worked at that have gotten fired. They could have avoided this by implementing the career best practice process of meeting every month or two with their supervisor and asking for feedback.

You need to ask for feedback from your boss in a one on one setting often. She or he will help to guide you to stay on the path to success. Ask what you need to do to add more value to the team or what you need to accomplish before getting promoted or before getting a raise.

If you don't ask for feedback often, then communication will break down and you could lose your job. Most people are surprised when they get fired. Over communicate when it comes to this topic.

Lesson #61: The Only Way to Get Promoted or a Raise

As counterintuitive as this might sound, you need to ask to get promoted. You also need to ask to get a raise. Most successful businesspeople that get promoted often and rise to the top asked to get to that level. It's very true.

You will get passed over for a promotion or a raise if you don't ask for it. Similar to the Steve Jobs chapter on asking, you need to ask for everything you want in life. Nobody is going to give you what you want unless you ask for it.

Your supervisor should be cool with this as she or he knows that you are trying to provide for your family. They have been in that position before too! In fact, they probably got promoted to their level because they asked.

If you feel very uncomfortable with this (you shouldn't), then phrase the question like this "I love working here and I love the team too. Can you please let me know what I need to accomplish or what value I need to add in order to get promoted or a raise?" Then once you achieve the goals or benchmarks that your supervisor gives you in response to your question, then remind him or her of your accomplishments after you achieve them and you will get the raise. It goes without saying that you should only approach your boss with this conversation when they are in a good mood or positive state.

LESSON #62: THERE IS A PLAN B BEFORE YOU QUIT

People often resign from a job because they found a better gig somewhere else or because they couldn't get the job they want in the company they currently work for. If you receive a job offer from another company with an awesome role and an amazing salary, before divulging this to your supervisor in your current role, ask him or her to help you get a better role internally. Chances are they will help you get this role.

You need to burn all bridges internally before resigning when you have an offer in hand. Heck you have nothing to lose anyway! If this approach doesn't work, then tell your supervisor that you are unfortunately resigning. Over 50% of the time your supervisor will not want to lose you and she or he will either give you the raise that you clearly deserve or help you get the role you want to receive internally. Your plan B is to get that job internally before resigning. If you don't ask you will never receive in life.

LESSON #63: AVOID THIS AT ALL COSTS

We all enjoy a good drink every now and then. Be careful with alcohol and business especially at corporate events. My grandfather used to tell me to order 7 Up in a glass with ice at parties as it looks like an alcohol based drink. Let others get wasted and make a fool of themselves. Your career is too important to you to let this drug ruin you.

I have even been in situations where a shark will get you a few drinks and then ask you questions about your thoughts on colleagues in a condescending way. Don't give in. As always, keep your cards close to your chest. I have seen people lose their jobs at corporate events with alcohol. Always be on you're A game.

Lesson #64: Don't Go Over Your Boss' head

As tempting as it might be, don't try too hard to impress your boss' boss. Why? Because your boss will feel threatened by you and, as a result, you will likely hurt your chances of getting promoted or getting a raise.

I cringed while writing this chapter as I loathe corporate politics. However, it goes without saying that early in your career you should be very careful about communicating too often with your boss' boss. If your boss' boss approaches you or emails you, then you probably need to tell your boss about the communication if they feel threatened by you. This will lead to perceived loyalty.

However, if you feel that you are going to get fired and that your boss is taking all of your credit anyway, then take a damn risk and meet with your boss' boss and let them know what your accomplishments are. Gutsy but a worthwhile move if needed.

LESSON #65: BE A NICE DUMB GUY

My uncle told me about being a nice dumb guy before I started my first job in the consulting industry. I had no idea what he was talking about. A decade later it all made sense. You don't want to be seen as a threat by your colleagues that might want to back stab you if they feel that you have a better chance of getting promoted than you do. I am not implying that you should be disingenuous, but when you are around these sharks be a nice dumb guy.

What the heck is Chris talking about? Well if people feel threatened by you, then how do you make sure that they don't feel threatened? Just chill out and don't try to impress them. Unfortunately you might need to also adopt this attitude if your boss feels threatened by you. It goes without saying in this case that you shouldn't be a nice dumb guy in front of your boss' boss for obvious reasons.

Lesson #66: Never Complain

There is no upside in having a negative attitude. Complainers destroy a corporate culture. Complainers make a lower salary. Complainers don't get promoted as often. What is the upside? There is no upside complaining in work or in life period.

Don't bring down your colleagues or your team mates. When they complain simply state something positive about the current situation that they are complaining about. You are helping them by doing this too. Find the positive in every situation and watch your career take off.

SECTION 12: ONLY TAKE ADVICE FROM SUCCESSFUL PEOPLE

It is Crucial that You Take Advice from the Right People

Lesson #67: You Need Yodas!

You need many Yodas in your life and in your career. You need mentors and you need to mentor others in order to reinforce what your core beliefs or critical career and success factors are.

Make sure that your Yodas (or mentors) are in a position that you want to be in one day. Are they successful professionally? Are they successful personally? Did they achieve a great work/life balance? Are some of their past accomplishments your future goals? Can you trust them? Do you enjoy their company? Can they offer you constructive criticism so that they can help you to seek continuous improvement?

It is extraordinarily rare for an executive to rise to the top of any organization or for any entrepreneur to be wildly successful without many mentors. Hewlett mentored Steve Jobs and Steve Jobs mentored Marc Benioff from Salesforce, which is now the largest employer in San Francisco.

People are flattered when you ask them to mentor you. They almost always say yes when you ask them. Ask and you shall receive mentors. They will help you achieve your goals in life.

LESSON #68: FOLLOW THESE PEEPS

I have always been a voracious reader of biographies of successful people. I love learning from them. What are their recipes for success? How did they do it? Did they lead a well-balanced life on the road to their success?

Although I am incredibly busy, I make time to learn from the best using www.Audible.com. I listen to many biographies of successful people in the car, in the shower and in the kitchen.

Use Twitter to follow your business heroes. They often tweet incredibly motivational quotes that resonate well with me. I love their short snippets of optimism, hope and best practices.

I find it incredibly motivating to know as much as I can about these successful people as most of them came from very uncompromising backgrounds. I love the poor, smart and hungry rags to riches stories. I feel empowered when thinking about them; there are no limits to what you can achieve. These people are no smarter than you are.

LESSON #69: I HAVE NEVER MET A SUCCESSFUL PERSON WITH...

You will never meet an extremely successful person with a negative attitude. If they didn't believe in themselves and in their goals, then they would never have been successful.

The quintessential example of this is Richard Branson. I just finished his latest audiobook and my goodness does he ever have an infectious positive attitude! In the 1970s when IBM and Digital said there is no market for personal computers, Bill Gates had a passion and a goal for a world where we would have a computer on every desk and in every home. Without this positive attitude there would be no Microsoft and the computer revolution would not have taken place.

One of my favorite movies is Tucker about a man (played by Jeff Bridges) that is so determined to succeed with the most positive attitude ever! Please watch Tucker and when you are feeling unmotivated say to yourself "Hold that tiger!"

LESSON #70: FOLLOW THE SMART MONEY

When you invest in companies or industries or sectors, a simple successful approach is to follow the smart money. Warren Buffett is incredibly successful so let's invest in some of the companies that he does.

I know that this section seems like common sense but if you invest in companies that smart money investors invest in then you will more often than not have a winning investing strategy.

Always be skeptical when a friend or a businessperson asks you to invest in a company that no name investors have already invested in. If you are in a situation like this, ask yourself a basic question which is "Why am I so lucky to be given this opportunity?" The reason, unfortunately, is because the smart money passed on this investment. You should pass on this investment as well.

SECTION 13: ONLY THE PARANOID SURVIVE

*It is **Crucial** to Be Paranoid About these Issues….*

LESSON #71: HIT THIS KEY AND LOSE YOUR JOB

Please triple check all emails before hitting the send button. This is especially true when emailing your boss or a client. There is no excuse for grammatical errors or ill thought out logic in electronic communications.

Your digital image is a reflection of your work ethic and professional standards. Don't be lazy when it comes to proof reading electronic communications.

I tell my kids to be extraordinarily careful with social networking too as each post can be accessed by anyone in the world forever. Don't think that you are not at risk using services like Snapchat or that you can always delete social media posts because you can't; electronic footprints are forever. Only the paranoid survive when it comes to digital communication.

LESSON #72: LET THIS SECRET OUT AND YOU ARE DONE

If you are ever considering leaving your company for any reason at some point, including to pursue a graduate degree, keep it to yourself. Why? Because most businesses are highly cyclical and during the next economic downturn management will need to let people go. The sharks will remind management that you aren't that committed because you were considering leaving to attend graduate school.

Large organizations tend to over hire and over fire; they often cut into muscle. If you give your boss or anyone the impression that you are not 100% long term committed then once the layoffs start, you are at risk. Keep it to yourself and your family/close friends if you are applying to business school or planning to leave the company to get another degree. Hopefully you start your graduate degree when a recession is starting as this is always the best time to be in school.

LESSON #73: DISASTER RECOVERY, YOUR PERSONAL BACKUP PLAN

Given how cyclical business can be and given how erratic your company can be from a human resources perspective, you need to always have a contingency plan or a plan B in place in case disaster strikes.

Earlier in my career I often got calls from head hunters. I took every single meeting just in case I needed a back-up plan. Forget about loyalty when it comes to your career or protecting your family. There is nothing unloyal about wanting to provide for your family. I am fortunate that I don't need to take these meetings at this point in my life but I took all of them in my 20s and 30s. In fact, one of these meetings got me the job of a lifetime despite the fact that I was happy where I was at that point in my life.

Having a contingency plan in place with a competitor or a firm in another industry is a smart personal and professional risk management best practice.

Lesson #74: Question Motives

You need to question everyone's motives in business. When you see financial pundits on television, they are there because they are pitching their product, service or "talking their book" which means they are pimping their stocks because they want you to buy them and drive up their net worth.

If you understand the actions of your competitors or your peers or your supervisors, then you will understand the purpose of their actions better and be able to appropriately react. I am not recommending that you be cynical in life, but understanding the motive of a business person's action will help you make better business decisions.

For example, are they overselling their products or services to me because they are at risk of missing their quarterly quotas? If so, I can squeeze them on margins and get a better price. Simply put yourself in their shoes and try to understand their actions so you can react accordingly.

SECTION 14: RISK TAKING

It is Crucial that You Take the Right Kinds of Risks

LESSON #75: FAIL FAST AND EARLY

It's important to take on a lot of career risk when you are younger and don't have kids. You can always recover quickly and bounce back. Potential employers might respect the fact that you are a self-starter, proactive and confident enough in your abilities to take a risk.

If you are young and you take a risk and fail then consider going to business school or at least applying once you start your company in order to have a backup plan. If you are not young and you start a company then give it 1-2 years max. If it doesn't succeed by then then you should consider failing fast and moving on to your plan B. Don't be emotionally attached to your company if you can't achieve your goals. Don't worry as you can always start another company at some point in your life. Success is merely a result of multiple perceived failures.

LESSON #76: O.P.M.

Good business ideas can always attract investors. If you don't have a significant amount of money in the bank, then please use Other People's Money (O.P.M.) to build your business. Don't put your family at risk. Don't ruin your credit score. Seek equity investors (not bank loans) to help you grow your business.

Don't use bank loans because banks are piranhas; if you miss one payment, then they will likely force you to default and they will seize your assets. If possible, please try to get high net worth or institutional investors to help you build your business. They can also help you tremendously when it comes to how to build your business if they are on your board or if they are advisors.

If you have questions on how to raise money, please search for my name (Chris Haroun) on www.udemy.com and take the course I created on fundraising.

LESSON #77: DON'T INVEST IF ALL OF THE FOUNDERS HAVE LEFT

I am a firm believer that you should never invest in a company when all the founders have resigned, especially in the technology sector. 99% of the time in tech, when a founder resigns, investors should run for the exits.

Founders don't care about corporate politics or bureaucracy; they get stuff done and they correctly don't give a damn what other people think. When a founder resigns, then politics take over. Executives are motivated by the ability to climb the corporate ladder. Executives are often politicians as they are all talk with no substance. Executives often feel that it doesn't make sense to take a risk and innovate with a new product because if they fail then their career is done and if they succeed then they aren't going to get paid anyway!

A company's success is based on the culture that the founder has created. If she or he resigns, then the culture will eventually become diluted and style drift will set in as will complacency. The company will then spin into an irreversible terminal secular decline.

For more details on this topic please go to www.VentureBeat.com and check out the article that I wrote on this topic including examples of companies that are successful because the founder(s) is(are) still there, including Amazon, Google and Salesforce.

SECTION 15: SALES BEST PRACTICES

The Best CEOs are the Best Salespeople. Learn these Crucial Sales Secrets.

LESSON #78: LESS IS MORE

Steve Jobs was the quintessential communicator and entrepreneur. He firmly believed that for a product or idea to be widely adopted, it needed to have a simplistic design. The iPhone and iPad have only one button. His presentations usually have 3 bullet points or 3 images per slide and that's all.

In this day and age we are so inundated with information that 144 character bottom line summaries are more relevant than lengthy write-ups. This is why Twitter has been so incredibly successful. The best business model presentations that I see as a venture capitalist have a maximum of 10 slides with only 3 bullet points per slide; less is more works.

Executives and potential investors have extraordinarily short attention spans in this day and age given the many screens that we are addicted to like smart phones, tablets, laptops, watches etc. You need to get your point across in as few words as possible.

Pretend that each message that you send costs you $100 per word. With this in mind you will definitely embrace the winning methodology of less is more.

For help on how to fundraise or how to build financial models using the less is more methodology, please go to www.Udemy.com and search on my name (Chris Haroun) and take my courses on the aforementioned subjects.

LESSON #79: PRESENT WITH PASSION & ENJOY PUBLIC SPEAKING

One of the most important skillsets that most business schools don't teach is how to give effective presentations. Effective presentations are ones where the presenter is speaking from the heart, with high energy and with a lot of passion! Watch Ted Talks or YouTube presentations by Steve Jobs or Marc Benioff or Ronald Reagan or Barrack Obama for superb examples of how to present.

Each slide needs to have as little information as possible on it. Remember that less is always more. You also need to use your hands a lot, make eye contact with everyone in the audience and use long pregnant pauses after you say something that is important.

Don't ever present for more than 10 minutes without a video, a funny image or a break as we can't pay attention for long periods of time; there is a reason that Ted Talks are less than 15 minutes.

Don't read a script. Rather, go off script and speak right from the heart. Story telling works, especially ones where you have a hero (your product) and a villain (the competitor's products). Apple is very effective with this; recall the "I am a Mac and I am a PC" commercials.

For help on how to present with passion and enjoy public speaking, please go to www.Udemy.com and search on my name (Chris Haroun) and take my course on presentations.

LESSON #80: SHUT UP IF YOU THINK YOU CLOSED THE SALE

One of the biggest mistakes people make in sales is that they oversell. If you do this, your buyer will think that there is something wrong with your product or that you are desperate to make the sale; caveat emptor. Once you think that the buyer wants the product then stop talking.

If you oversell then the buyer might see blood in the water and talk your pricing point down and destroy your margins or commissions. More than often they will simply not buy your product.

Remember that your product or service is so awesome that you don't need this sale anyway as you are selling a premium product that commands higher prices than the competition. How many commercials do you recall seeing for premium products like Tiffany's or Coach versus McDonald's or Wal-Mart?

Your customer needs your product and you are helping them by giving them the opportunity to purchase the product. Don't ever oversell. Once you sense that they are committed to purchasing your product, simply shut up.

Lesson #81: Small Clients are Just as Much Work as Big Clients

Don't waste your time trying to get small clients. Elephant hunt. You will find that small customers are just as much work and often more work than large customers!

Why is this the case? Smaller customers usually have less disposable income and, as a result, are more likely to want to return the product or pester you with too many customer support questions. Larger clients, by contrast, can be more sophisticated so they require less customer support and they also likely have less of their net worth invested in your product.

Don't get me wrong as you need to respect and appreciate all customers in business, but your time is valuable and it would be nice to spend less time servicing smaller customers and more time working on new leads or more time with your family. Life is too short.

LESSON #82: ALL I HEARD WAS NOT NO

I am good friends with a CEO who I believe is the best salesperson I have ever met as he is very similar to Marc Benioff. In fact, all great CEOs are great salespeople. The best salespeople are relentless until the customer expresses interested in the product they are selling or, more importantly, until they hear no.

You have not failed at selling your product or service until the prospect says no. Until then, keep trying different angles to sell your product or service. Be creative and don't ever give up on this lead until she or he says no. Until then, all you heard was "not no".

:)

LESSON #83: TALK BUSINESS LATER

Your best customers can become great friends of yours. Get to know them well before conducting business. Ask them were they are form, what they love in life. Create a personal bond with them. I have the luxury of only dealing with clients that I like a lot. You will get to a point in your career when you can chose your customers and enjoy their company.

Don't talk business until you get to know your customer or business partners. The topic of this chapter might sound redundant given the section of this book on Relationships are More Important than Product Knowledge, but getting to know your customers first before talking business is always prudent.

Once you understand who your customers are and what their needs are, you can tailor your product or service to fit their needs and help them with their goals. You need to genuinely believe that your product or service will help them achieve their goals by either helping them make more money or helping them to save money.

LESSON #84: HOW TO GET A MEETING WITH ANYONE

Sales is all about meeting people. How do you get meetings? What do you do once you get those meetings? Where do I start?

In this day and age, the best resource on the planet for getting meetings is LinkedIn. I simply cannot say enough positive things about this social media gold mine.

My success rate in getting meetings with people that I have never met before using LinkedIn is 95%. I don't say this to impress you; rather, I say this to impress upon you the fact that you can do it too.

Here are the steps to getting a meeting with anyone:

1: Create your LinkedIn profile and make sure that you are connected with everyone you have ever met in your life. Don't ever connect with people that you have not met.

2: Sign up for the LinkedIn premium service. It doesn't cost that much and I promise you that it is a worthwhile investment. I think that you can even try it for free for a month.

3: Click on "advanced search".

4: Do a search for people that have something in common with you. Search for those that went to the same school as you did. Alternatively, search for people that live in your zip code (or the zip code you will be visiting) that are from the same home town or country that you are from. Alternatively, search for people that are in the same clubs or associations that you are a part of.

5: In LinkedIn, create an "inMail" with the category section of "Expertise Request". For the subject line of the inMail, enter "Hi". The contents of the inMail message should be short and polite; remember that less is more and that gratitude is important. The inMail message should mention what you have in common and should not mention why you want to meet. Here are 2 examples of effective inMails:

> John,
>
> Hope all is well. I am also a graduate of McGill University and I also live in the Bay Area. Please let me know if you have time for a coffee in the next few weeks.
>
> Thanks a lot,
> Chris

> John,
>
> Hope all is well. I am also from Mississauga and I will be in the Bay Area for all of next month. Please let me know if you have time for a coffee.
>
> Thanks a lot,
> Chris

Please keep in mind that people from similar backgrounds want to help you. The farther away you and the inMail prospect are from home, the more they want to help you. You just need to ask!

You can also consider asking a friend of yours in LinkedIn to introduce you to one of their contacts. Again, please make sure to add every person you meet in your life from now on to LinkedIn as your success in business is partially predicated on the quality and number of relationships that you have.

The beautiful thing about networking for getting meetings using LinkedIn inMails instead of cold calling or using email is that not many people do it...yet. Embrace it and enjoy meeting new people!

LESSON #85: CONFIDENCE LEADS TO COMPETENCE

Please don't confuse confidence with arrogance but if you are confident and humble, people will think you are competent and likeable at the same time.

I recently wrote an article in www.AlleyWatch.com on confidence. The article was controversial as the crux of the message was that American students, regardless of what country they were born in are number one in the world when it comes to confidence. Confidence leads to great sales skills. Great sales skills leads to the ability to raise money. The ability to raise money leads to the ability to create companies. The ability to create companies leads to the ability to innovate and disrupt industries like Uber and Airbnb have, etc.

You need to come across as confident when you are selling your product and service as perceived confidence more often than not leads to perceived competence, which should help you increase your selling success rate.

LESSON #86: SPORTS IS CRUCIAL BOARDROOM TALK

I am absolutely passionate about baseball. I love my Toronto Blue Jays; I always have been since I was a kid. It's a big part of who I am and what I love in life. It is the bond that bring my family and friends together as we all share a common love for the Blue Jays. For me, it's hard not to be romantic about baseball.

When I meet new people, if they are from a city with a Major League Baseball team I always ask them if they are a baseball fan. If they are from Boston I ask them about Big Pappi who everybody loves. If they are from New York, I ask them about Derek Jeter, who is the quintessential role model for all kids, including my oldest son. If I meet someone from Pittsburgh, I mention Roberto Clemente who is the biggest hero ever given the sacrifice he endured the month after his 3000th hit.

Sports talk is bonding talk and I truly love it. I love getting to know new people that I meet by talking about baseball. If your passion is soccer or football, then talk about these wonderful sports in the boardroom or anywhere else. By talking about sports you learn a lot about people, including where they are from and what they are passionate about. On the second or third or fiftieth meeting I have with anyone that I have ever met that is from a different city and also loves baseball, this is the first thing we always talk about. I am excited just writing about this section… :)

LESSON #87: GOLF OFTEN

I suck at golf. If I can break 100 I am happy. It doesn't matter though because I golf because I love meeting people, having fun and learning about them. Many chapters in this book were inspired by business tycoons that I have golfed with and asked about why they are successful while we are playing golf.

Golf is so relaxing too. I love getting to know business partners, customers, supervisors and strangers while playing golf. You certainly don't have to be good at golf to leverage it as the best sales tool ever, you just have to enjoy people.

There is no better event in sales for getting to know potential customers well than golf. Enjoy it and embrace it.

LESSON #88: DRESS FOR SUCCESS

Be the woman or man you want to become. The way you carry yourself is the way others will treat you. People will respect you if take the time to dress well.

Dress the way a person would one level above you in your job. If you take time to look good, people will think you are confident and hence competent. There is no excuse for looking like a slob; you do have time to get ready or find the right clothes to wear.

An executive or salesperson that dresses like a slob is perceived to be less reliable, dependable and less successful. If you don't know what to wear for a job interview, go to the company's website and look at picture of what they are wearing. Alternatively, go to LinkedIn and look at the profile pictures of the people that are going to interview you and dress in line with their style. Dress well and excel.

LESSON #89: LEVERAGE THE MEDIA

I have always found that most successful companies don't have the best products; rather, they have the best marketing skills. Microsoft Windows was never the best operating system, but the company had superb media and marketing skills.

The most successful executives are constantly in the media as they see this as free advertising for their product and service. I love watching Richard Branson and Marc Benioff on television conducting interviews because they are incredibly inspirational. Their genius though is partially through leveraging the media to evangelize their companies. Richard Branson did this by literally driving a tank through New York's Times Square. Another great example has been Marc Benioff getting any reason he can get to be interviewed and explain why traditional client server software products are dead and why cloud computing and Salesforce are revolutionary productivity tools. Embrace the media.

SECTION 16: THINK DIFFERENT

Crucial Highly Profitable Differentiation Strategies

Lesson #90: Be a Contrarian and Watch Your Net Worth Soar

Warren Buffett famously said "be greedy when others are fearful and fearful when others are greedy." Buffett has made billions doing the opposite of what other investors do! It's not rocket science: if everybody is buying a stock, then the price is too high and you won't make money; the converse is of course true as well.

I tell my kids the same things when it comes to their baseball cards. I tell them to sell them when everybody wants them and buy the great players' cards when nobody wants them. I was proud of my son when he sold a Chris Bryant rookie card for $25. I wish I had done the same when I was young with my cards!

The same lesson can be applied with any investment in life. Please be patient as I promise you will likely have a chance at some point to buy the investment that you want to buy at a cheaper pricing point. The same can be said for any product you buy online; just be patient and wait for it to go on sale!

LESSON #91: BIG COMPANIES CAN'T INNOVATE

Do you ever wonder why big companies can't seem to innovate? Why is it that large companies like Microsoft are less relevant today? Ford created the car but heck what ground breaking innovations have they released lately?

The rule of thumb is that large companies simply can't innovate if the founder is no longer at the company. That's right. What about Amazon, aren't they innovative? Yes they are and the founder Jeff Bezos is still running the company. In fact, Amazon still runs today like a small company. Bezos doesn't let any meeting take place at Amazon that requires more than 2 pizzas to feed the team.

Make sure you don't have too many cooks in the kitchen. We have all had the unpleasant experience of having too many people on a group project; it's an unmitigated disaster! Whenever I invest in venture capital in a start-up I am never concerned about competition from a large company. I am always concerned about competition from a few women or men in a garage are plotting to "Uber" or "Airbnb" the industry they are competing in.

Small groups of people can change the world. Big groups of people are called governments and highly ineffective at innovation given the nature of corporate politics.

Lesson #92: Form Your Own Opinions Dummy

Always form your own opinions in business. In your mind, question everything. Do your own work before deciding whether or not to make an investment or make a critical business decision.

You don't need a fast talking confident Wall Street analyst on TV to tell you how to invest your money. You don't need a financial planner that has a mediocre net worth to tell you how to preserve your capital. You don't need a cocky colleague at work to tell you what business decisions to make or how to manage your career. You don't need a Harvard MBA consultant to tell you what your next business move should be.

Do your own homework and do your own due diligence in business. Remember that YOU are the smartest person in the world.

LESSON #93: TAKE THAT WALK!

Some of the best decisions in life are made on long walks. Steve Jobs used to go on long walks with his friend, Oracle founder Larry Ellison. All US Presidents needed R&R at Camp David to go on long walks to come up with impactful decisions.

Go on at least one long walk per week in order to clear your thoughts and assess where you are in life. When you have a critical decision that needs to be made in life, take a long walk and decide what to do.

When I worked in the consulting industry, I wasn't passionate about what I was doing and I thought maybe an MBA might help? I played a round of golf alone and in between holes, I wrote down the pros and cons on going to business school on two separate pieces of paper. I then put a score out of ten next to each criteria; 10 was the highest score and 1 was the lowest score. I then added up the scores. The total score on the pros card outweighed the total score on the cons page.

That long walk on the golf course that day in 1997 changed my life.

LESSON #94: PASSION FOR PLATFORMS

The best investments and companies to start are the ones that have the largest total addressable markets or T.A.Ms. Don't ever start a company that has a small T.A.M. because in the highly unlikely event that you capture 95% of this market, you won't be putting a dent in the universe.

So what are the best types of companies to start or invest in (assuming the management team is stellar)? Platforms rock. Platforms are the best investments you can make. What some examples of platforms? EBay is the largest auction platform. Microsoft Windows is the largest computing platform. LinkedIn is the largest human resources platform. Facebook is the largest consumer social media platform. Uber is the largest taxi platform. Airbnb is the largest hotel platform. Salesforce is the largest customer relationship management cloud platform. Udemy is the largest online education platform.

The best investments are the ones where the company owns the roads and the users or customers are like tollbooths or autos. Let the users do the hard work of building out the platform.

LESSON #95: DON'T RESPECT TRADITION, RESPECT INNOVATION

Given the ubiquitous nature of broadband computing and given the torrid growth of cloud computing, all traditional business models are at risk of being disrupted. Respect innovation and not business tradition.

We live in interesting times. Relatively new companies like Uber and Airbnb are disrupting 100 year old companies. Tradition and business is like oil and vinegar, they won't mix well. I am particularly bullish on investing in innovation and not in traditional business models. We are on the cusp of the most revolutionary disruptive business model discoveries in the history of the world. I couldn't be more excited about the pipeline of innovation in front of us.

When assessing business models, it's important to always consider how the underlying company could get disrupted if computing resources are virtually free, which is going to happen relatively soon.

For more details on this topic, please see the www.Wired.com and www.Entrepreneur.com articles that I have written on these topics.

SECTION 17: YOU BE YOU

*It is **Crucial** to Find YOUR Passion*

LESSON #96: BE HONEST AND SPEAK FROM THE HEART

People love honesty and humility. When presenting or participating in meetings, be yourself and speak right from the heart. Throw out that script and don't be artificial.

I will never forget when I was a teenager in the 1980s the late great Ronald Reagan gave the most prophetic speech I have ever seen. He was speaking in front of the Berlin Wall and he went off script and with a few words changed the world. He said "Mr. Gorbachev tear down this wall!" I get shivers just thinking of that epic moment in time. You can hear Reagan's passion when he went off script and spoke right from the heart.

Be honest with yourself and your family and throw down a challenge by letting them and yourself know what you are most passionate about in life. Speak from your heart and tell them your passion. If you have a job you are doing it wrong. Find your passion and you will never work a day in your life.

LESSON #97: LISTEN TO YOUR SPOUSE

Behind almost every single successful business person is a great spouse. You are a team and you have likely only gotten to where you are in life because of their mentoring. Listen to them and thank them often. I often read my emails that I am composing to my wife Christine before sending them. Her feedback always rocks.

Your spouse knows what makes you happy in business. Remind them often what your business passions are. In return, they will remind you what you love in life and reinforce and hence help guide and remind you what you are on this earth to accomplish in business. What is your purpose?

Your spouse is your ultimate confidant and life coach. Only your spouse can tell you if what you are wearing went out of style 80 years ago! Only your spouse can tell you that you sound too arrogant when practicing a corporate presentation. Only your spouse can remind you why you wanted to work in the industry you work in. Only your spouse can help you achieve your long term goals. So thank your spouse often as you will never get a better life coach.

Lesson #98: Don't Let Anyone Rent Space in Your Head

Don't let your upcoming success get sabotaged by the doubters. Don't let those with inferior expectations of themselves destroy your confidence in yourself and your goals/ambitions. Don't let anyone rent space in your head.

At this point in the book, it goes without saying that you should only surround yourself with people that are positive and want you to succeed. It goes without saying that you are the smartest person in the world. It goes without saying that there are no goals in life that you cannot achieve.

A warning worth mentioning is that you (yes you) are your biggest critic. Don't let that critic rent space in your head either. Please always stay confident in your abilities and if you need a pep talk have your spouse or your good friends that also have lofty goals remind you of what you are going to accomplish in life. In times of self-doubt, read the goals you have written down. If you have not yet written down your goals start right now and I mean right now. Write down 10 business goals right now that you are going to accomplish in your life and don't be conservative.

LESSON #99: TAKE TIME FOR YOU, DAMMIT!

I know that the type of person that is reading this book is always focused on continuous improvement. I know that the type of person that is reading this book has high expectations and lofty goals. I know that the type of person that is reading this book spends way more time helping other people and not themselves.

Please take time for yourself too; help yourself. Enjoy the finer things in life that bring joy to your life. Why would I write that in a book on business lessons? Because if you are happy personally then you will be much more successful professionally and you will set much higher goals. It is important that you stop to smell the roses every now and then.

:)

Lesson #100: You Are Never Too Old to Start Over

When I was a kid I remember seeing commercials for Freedom 55, which was a retirement savings company. Then as I got older, this age became 65 for those eligible to receive social security benefits. This age is slowly increasing. It's ludicrous that people retire in their 60s or 70s. Heck, I know of many people in their 80s that are much sharper than I am.

We are on the cusp of a biotech and healthcare renaissance were we will see the eradication of many diseases in the next few decades. I think most people alive today will live to be more than 100 if they take care of themselves. I know in my heart that at some point in my life people will live to 150+ years old.

With this in mind, why would you want to retire in your 60s when you have another 100 potential years? You are never too old to start a new career or start a new company. Anybody that thinks otherwise is guilty in my humble opinion of age discrimination. It doesn't matter how old or young you are, leverage your network and reinvent yourself over and over again until you find your passion!

LESSON #101: FRUSTRATION LEADS TO REINVENTION

If you have a high level of professional frustration in your life then this is a gift to you. It's a gift to you because you are not professionally doing what you are most passionate about.

It's perfectly normal to be frustrated in business. The fun part is figuring out what you love doing in life and what your business purpose is in life. What were you put on this earth to accomplish professionally? How many lives could you help improve if you accomplished your business goals? What would it take for you to no longer feel professionally frustrated?

Frustration leads to breakthroughs.

Frustration leads to reinvention.

Find your professional passion and end your frustration; welcome to the new you.

Closing Remarks

Thank you. I hope you have enjoyed *101 Crucial Lessons they Don't Teach You in Business School* by Chris Haroun.

If you are interested in taking online courses taught by Chris Haroun please visit: www.Udemy.com/user/chris-haroun/.

Please see Chris Haroun's latest publication which is available on Amazon and Kindle, called:

> "The Ultimate Practical Business Manual
> Everything You Need to Know About Business
> (from Launching a Company to Taking it Public)"

If you would like to receive articles and blogs written by Chris Haroun or if you are interested in having Chris as a guest speaker at your school, charity or company, please contact or submit your email address at:
www.BusinessCareerCoaching.com.

Made in the USA
San Bernardino, CA
05 October 2016